JESUS SECOND COMING AND HAMONAH

By: Leif Krogstad

**SOON THE LAST TRUMPHET WILL SOUND AND THAT
PROCLAIM THE SECOND COMING OF JESUS CHRIST AND
THEY WILL ALL WHO HAS FOLLOWED JESUS HERE MEET
HIM WHEN HE COMES UP IN THE SKY AND BE IN HEAVEN
FOR ALL TIME. AMEN**

**ALSO Last in Ezekiel 37 a.s.o. it is descriebed a war
against Israel – all nations going to be a part of it but main
is Russia and EU – EU is the Beast in Revelation book of
John – it got a deadly wound when Adolph Hitler lost the
war – he killed 6 million Jews – the pearl in the eye of God
– and Germany never is forgiven for that and shall be
punished – but that wound got healed by the unification of
the evil Germany in 1990 by this unification. Israel is
going to use all their atom weapons in this war it is written
that the Israeli people is going to defend themselves by
weapons of fluel. At the same time Jesus do return and we
who are Christians going to meet him up in the sky and the
world will burn down and a new earth and a new heaven
will appear where rightoesness do rule for all time and we
are going to live in the New Jerusalem for all time. Russia**

1

is Gog and Magog and Meshek and Tubal all places in Russia. The Pope really is the false prophet in Revelation book – He is in Hell and religon is his tool. Evil tool. The product of him evil work. As we can see in Revelation book the last thing happening is that the false prophet and his tool is thrown in Gahenna by the King riding the white horse. At The Catholic Church is the Bitch in Revalation book.

And soon our King Jesus Christ is going return to judge all flesh – all human kind as King and judge at judgment day – when he do close the age and we the Kingdom of Heaven fore all eternity. The New Jerusalem to inherit fore eternity to come no end of it. And meet all our beloved ones there. Then the King of Kings will say: Now the time is closed! God bless you all here mentioned and who is not none forgotten. Very soon now Jesus is going to return and that is the end of the end.

"And I saw, and behold a white horse: and he that sat on him had a bow; and a crown was given unto him: and he went forth conquering, and to conquer. And I saw heaven opened, and behold a white horse; and he that sat upon him was called Faithful and True, and in righteousness he doth judge and make war. And the He fought agains the False Prophet at last - and the False Prophet was thrown in Gahenna... And the rest of them were all killed with the sword of fire in the hand by King riding the white horse.

Then I saw a great white throne and the King of Kings was seated on and crowned he is and - and each person was jugded according to what they had done.... And the devil was thrown into the lake of eternal fire and eternal suffer... Then death and Hades were thrown in the lake of fire... And if anyone's name was not found, he was thrown into the lake of fire and eternal suffer forever devided from God's people..."

Quote: Matthew: Jesus Christ: "So don't be affraid of them. There are nothing conceailed that will not be disclosed, or hidden that will not be made known. What I do tell you in the dark, speak it in daylight; what is whispered in your ear, proclaim it from the roofs!" "I did not come to bring peace, but a sword. For it I come to turn!" "If anyone won't welcome you or listen your words, shake the dust off your feet; when you leave that home or town. I tell you truely; it will be more bearable fore Sodom and Gomorrah on the day of judgement then fore that town

Quotes from The Holy Bible.

IT IS WRITTEN IN HOLY BIBLE ABOUT IT ALSO IN EZKIEL WHERE IT ALSO IS PROPHESIES ABOUT THE USA AS THE WHITE HORSE (REVELATION BOOK) THAT JESUS CHRIST IS RIDING WITH A SWORD IN HIS HAND - OF FIRE - ANIMALS ARE ALWAYS COUNTRIES OR EMPIRES OR LOCATIONS AS MENTIONED IN JEWISH BIBLE IN EZRAS THIRD BOOK - IT IS THEN MENTIONED A BIG BEAST IT

WAS NAZI GERMANY BUT IT IS ALSO MENTIONED AFTER
THAT A LITTLE BEAST THAT SHALL TAKE POWER FROM
THE BIG BEAST AND COME OUT OF THE EARTH. BUT IN
EZEKIEL IS WRITTEN TAKE ONE STICK OF WOOD AND
WRITE ON IT BELONG TO JUDA TRIBE AND PUT IT IN
YOUR RIGHT HAND AND TAKE THEN AN OTHER STICK OF
WOOD AND WRITE ON IN BELONG TO JOSEPH TRIBE AND
PUT IN YOUR LEFT HAND THEN JOIN THEM TOGETHER
SO THEY GET ONE STICK OF WOOD IN YOUR HAND. THE
MEANING OF THIS IS THAT THE USA AS JOSEPH TRIBE
SHALL BE JOINED TOGETHER WITH ISRAEL - JUDA TRIBE
- AND THEY BECOME JESUS CHRIST'S HEAVENLY
KINGDOM. IN EZEKIEL IS ALSO WRITTEN ABOUT THE
COMING THEN ARMANGEDDON - IT IS TUBAL AND
MESHEC THAT IS NAMES OF RUSSIA AND RUSSIA SHALL
GO TO ATTACK AGAINST THIS UNIFICATION - THE
RESULT WILL BE THAT THEY WILL BE ATTACKED BY
WEAPONS OF FIRE AS WRITTEN IN EZEKIEL - BY THE
JEWISH PEOPLE AND BURN FOR ALL TIME IN THE LAKE
OF FIRE AND IN ADD IT IS MENTIONED THERE SHALL
ALSO BE A TOWN THERE NAMED: HAMONAH.

IT IS WRITTEN IN HOLY BIBLE ABOUT IT ALSO IN EZKIEL
WHERE IT ALSO IS PROPHESIES ABOUT THE USA AS THE
WHITE HORSE (REVELATION BOOK) THAT JESUS CHRIST
IS RIDING WITH A SWORD IN HIS HAND - OF FIRE -
ANIMALS ARE ALWAYS COUNTRIES OR EMPIRES OR
LOCATIONS AS MENTIONED IN JEWISH BIBLE IN EZRAS
THIRD BOOK - IT IS THEN MENTIONED A BIG BEAST IT

WAS NAZI GERMANY BUT IT IS ALSO MENTIONED AFTER THAT A LITTLE BEAST THAT SHALL TAKE POWER FROM THE BIG BEAST AND COME OUT OF THE EARTH. BUT IN EZEKIEL IS WRITTEN TAKE ONE STICK OF WOOD AND WRITE ON IT BELONG TO JUDA TRIBE AND PUT IT IN YOUR RIGHT HAND AND TAKE THEN AN OTHER STICK OF WOOD AND WRITE ON IN BELONG TO JOSEPH TRIBE AND PUT IN YOUR LEFT HAND THEN JOIN THEM TOGETHER SO THEY GET ONE STICK OF WOOD IN YOUR HAND. THE MEANING OF THIS IS THAT THE USA AS JOSEPH TRIBE SHALL BE JOINED TOGETHER WITH ISRAEL - JUDA TRIBE - AND THEY BECOME JESUS CHRIST'S HEAVENLY KINGDOM. IN EZEKIEL IS ALSO WRITTEN ABOUT THE COMING THEN ARMANGEDDON - IT IS TUBAL AND MESHEC THAT IS NAMES OF RUSSIA AND RUSSIA SHALL GO TO ATTACK AGAINST THIS UNIFICATION - THE RESULT WILL BE THAT THEY WILL BE ATTACKED BY WEAPONS OF FIRE AS WRITTEN IN EZEKIEL - BY THE JEWISH PEOPLE AND BURN FOR ALL TIME IN THE LAKE OF FIRE AND IN ADD IT IS MENTIONED THERE SHALL ALSO BE A TOWN THERE NAMED: HAMONAH - WHAT THE MEANING BY THIS IS; IS THAT IT SHALL BE A TOWN THAT SHALL BE THE BOARDERS AROUND THE THEN CREATED HELL - HELL IS IN THE LAKE OF FIRE - AND RUSSIA SHALL BE THERE AND AROUND THAT A TOWN NAMED HAMONAH. THE WHOLE PLACE OF ETERNAL PAIN IS NAMED IN EZEKIEL AS THE WALLEY OF HAMON. THAT WAS FROM THE HOLY BIBLE PARTS TELLING ABOUT THE SOON RETURN OF JESUS CHRIST - MESSAIAH.

ISRAEL IS GOING TO BE ATTACKED BY MANY NATIONS INCL. RUSSIA - AND IT GOING TO END UP IN ARMANGEDDON SOON TO COME. AND JESUS DO SAY HIMSELF IN MATTHEW THAT HE IS GOING FIRST TO DEVIDE NATIONS AND ONLY TWO IS GOING TO BE DEVIDED FROM THE REST THE REST END IN HAMON - THE LAKE OF FIRE" - BY DROPS OF HYDROGENIC BOMBS FROM ISRAEL. IS ALSO WRITTEN IN ISIAHA; "FROM NOW I THE LORD DO CREATE SOMETHING NEW - DON'T YOU RECOGNIZE IT; IT IS ALREADY GROWING UP.ALSO IT IS WRITTEN IN PETERS SECOND LETTER: "THE FIRST TIME THE WORLD SHALL BE PUNISHED BY WATER THE SECOND TIME BY FIRE!" - AND JESUS ALSO SAYS IN MATTHEW:"WHEN THE SON OF MAN IN THE HEAVEN WITH ALL HIS ANGELS AND SAVED THE UNIVERSE FORCES SHALL BE ROCKED AND THE STARS SHALL ALL FALL DOWN - AND THE SUN SHALL TURN WAY AND THE MOON SHALL TURN TO BLOOD"

"HEAVEN AND EARTH SHALL BOTH DISAPPEAR BUT MY WORDS SHALL ALWAYS BE"

"THEN IT SHALL APPEAR A WHITE THRONE WITH A KING JESUS CHRIST SITTING ON IT WITH A SWORD OF FIRE IN HIS RIGHT HAND AND WITH THAT SHALL SET A DOOM

OWER BOTH LIVING AND DEAD - THEY ON LEFT SIDE OF
HIM HE SHALL STRIKE WITH THE SWORD OF FIRE AND
THROUGH THEM ALL IN HELL TOGETHER WITH HITLER
THE FALSE PROPHET (THE POPE) AND WITH SATAN AND
HIS ANGELS AND BURN THERE IN ETERNAL SUFFER FOR
ALL TIME TO COME NO EVER END OF IT FOR EVER BURN
IN THE LAKE OF FIRE HAMON. AND ALSO A TOWN SHALL
BE THERE NAMED: HAMONAH

AMEN.

ZERO POINT ONE ZERO POINT ZERO - POINT ZERO - ONE
POINT ZERO= THE END OF THE END - THE ARMANGEDON -
NOW COMPARE EZEKIEL IN THE HOLY BIBLE.

IT IS THEN MENTIONED A BIG BEAST IT WAS NAZI
GERMANY BUT IT IS ALSO MENTIONED AFTER THAT A
LITTLE BEAST THAT SHALL TAKE POWER FROM THE BIG
BEAST AND COME OUT OF THE EARTH. IN EZEKIEL IS
ALSO WRITTEN ABOUT THE COMING THEN
ARMANGEDDON - IT IS TUBAL AND MESHEC THAT IS
NAMES OF RUSSIA AND RUSSIA SHALL GO TO ATTACK
AGAINST THIS UNIFICATION - THE RESULT WILL BE THAT
THEY WILL BE ATTACKED BY WEAPONS OF FIRE AS

WRITTEN IN EZEKIEL - BY THE JEWISH PEOPLE AND BURN FOR ALL TIME IN THE LAKE OF FIRE AND IN ADD IT IS MENTIONED THERE SHALL ALSO BE A TOWN THERE NAMED: HAMONAH - WHAT THE MEANING BY THIS IS IS THAT IT SHALL BE A TOWN THAT SHALL BE THE BOARDERS AROUND THE THEN CREATED HELL - HELL IS IN THE LAKE OF FIRE - AND RUSSIA SHALL BE THERE AND AROUND THAT A TOWN NAMED HAMONAH. THE WHOLE PLACE OF ETERNAL PAIN IS NAMED IN EZEKIEL AS THE WALLEY OF HAMON. THAT WAS FROM THE HOLY BIBLE PARTS TELLING ABOUT THE SOON RETURN OF JESUS CHRIST - MESSAIAH.

THAT IS THE END OF THE END AFTER THAT THE STARS SHALL FALL DOWN FROM HEAVEN AND SUN TURN AWAY AND MOON TOO - AND THE SIGN OF JUSUS CHRIST THE HOLY CROSS WILL APPEAR IN THE SKY. THEN JESUS CHRIST COMES VISIABLE FORE ALL FLESH AND THE PARADISE THEN AFTER THE DOOM BE REALITY FORE ALL TIME.   THAT IS THE WHOLE STORY TO COME IN NEAR FUTURE. NO TIME LIMIT ALMOST. GOD WILL ALWAYS ETERNELY BLESS ISRAEL! JESUS CHRIST OUR LORD IS UNDER RETURN AND WILL CLOSE THE TIME AND THE HEAVENLY KINGDOM FORE GOD'S CHILDREN TO INHERIT NOW VERY SOON. JUST SOME FEW PARTS LEFT IN ALL PROPHESIES GIVEN IN HOLY BIBLE LEFT. ALL THE AGES BE CLOSED BY JESUS CHRIST HIM SELF AS HE HAS PROMISED TO DO THEN. "AND LOOK I AM WITH YOU ALL THE AGES UNTIL I CLOSE THE AGE!" QUOTE: JESUS

CHRIST MATTHEW. "BLESSED BE THOSE WHO DO BLESS YOU: ISRAEL!"

THE END OF THE END THE EMPIRE OF JESUS CHIRST TO COME - SOON!

"And I saw a Beast coming out of sea.... That beast was killed and thrown in the Lake of fire and by the King riding the white horse – but is then following setting "And then I saw an other beast, coming out of the earth" – the power the last beast has it takes from the first – and the King riding the white horse did destroy also this last beast and throw it all in the lake of fire where the first beast already is and Anti Christ also just one thing left then to take the beast that came out of earth and then create the complete work – command to do so by Jesus Christ – at last after the doom set. The King on the white horse: Jesus Christ - by command: "Devide et impera" – then this little part – the little beast on earth be all thrown in Hell and creation of Hell fore all evil creatures to be for all time in eternal pain and punishement – no ever end of it when the last beast killed and the Devil who do rules that last location as a country or a city be determinated for all time all of it fore all time to come by the sword of fire in the hand of the King of Kings Jesus Christ. " "Concerning the coming of the Lord Jesus Christ , that day will not come until the rebellion occurs and the man of lawlessness is revealed, the man doomed to destruction. He will oppose and will exalt himself over that is named God or us worshipped - and even proclaim himself to be God!" "And now you can know who is holding him back, so he may be revealed at the proper time. Fore the secret power of the lawlessness is already at work. And then the lawless one will be revealed; whom the Lord Jesus will overthrow complete - determinate. The grace of our Lord Jesus Christ be with you all and defend you in the power of God's Holy Spirit. (2 Thes. 2)Then only one word left fore the King to say: "The Heavenly Kingom is now completed and it is just fore you be children and to take part of your herritage that been prepared fore you before the creation itself!" And at very last Jesus then will say one setting. "The Heavnly kingdom of the King Jesus Christ is now closed!" to be ruled by him the everlasting Heavenly Empire with Iron hand for all time – no end no beginning really had. God and Jesus always has ruled all there is. "

"And soon our King Jesus Christ is going return to judge all flesh – all human kind as King and judge at judgment day – when he do close the age and we the Kingdom of Heaven fore all eternity. The New Jerusalem to inherit fore eternity to come no end of it. And meet all our beloved ones there. Then the King of Kings will say: Now the time is closed! God bless you all here mentioned and who is not none forgotten. God bless the USA – the Heavenly Kingdom to come very soon in no time limit. Jesus Christ's Heavenly final Empire to be ruled by iron hand and mercy fore all time to come. Very soon now Jesus is going to return and that is the end of the end.".

THE END OF THE END THE EMPIRE OF JESUS CHIRST TO COME – SOON

"And I saw a Beast coming out of sea.... That beast was killed and thrown in the Lake of fire and by the King riding the white horse – but is then following setting "And then I saw an other beast, coming out of the earth" – the power the last beast has it takes from the first – and the king riding the white horse did destroy also this last beast and thrown it all in the lake of fire where the first beast already is and Anti Christ also just one thing left then to take the beast that came out of earth and then create the complete work – command to do so by Jesus Christ – at last after the doom set. The King on the white horse: Jesus Christ - by command: "Divide et impera" – then this little part – the little beast on earth be all thrown in Hell and creation of Hell fore all evil creatures to be for all time in eternal pain and punishment – no ever end of it when the last beast killed and the Devil who do rules that last location as a country or as in this case a city be determinated for all time all of it fore all time to come by the sword of fire in the hand of the King of Kings Jesus Christ – then only one word left fore the King do say: "The Heavenly Kingdom is now completed and it is just fore you be children to take part of your heritage that been prepared fore you before the creation itself!" And at very last Jesus then will say one setting. "The Heavenly kingdom of the King Jesus Christ is now closed!" to be ruled by him the everlasting Heavenly Empire with Iron hand for all time – no end no beginning really had. God and Jesus always has ruled all there is.

THE END OF THE END THE EMPIRE OF JESUS CHIRST TO COME - SOON!

"Fore the secret power of lawlessness is already in work". It is itself the very last part to have that closed fore all time."

And I saw, and behold a white horse: and he that sat on him had a bow; and a crown was given unto him: and he went forth conquering, and to conquer. And I saw heaven opened, and behold a white horse; and he that sat upon him was called Faithful and True, and in righteousness he doth judge and make war. And the He fought against the False Prophet at last - and the False Prophet was thrown in Gahenna... And the rest of them were all killed with the sword of fire in the hand by King riding the white horse. Then I saw a great white throne and the King of Kings was seated on and crowned he is and - and each person was judged according to what they had done.... And the devil was thrown into the lake of eternal fire and eternal suffer... The death and Hades were thrown in the lake of fire... And if anyone's name was not found, he was thrown into the lake of fire and eternal suffer forever divided from God's people...

Quote: Matthew: Jesus Christ: "So don't be afraid of them. There are nothing concealed that will not be disclosed, or hidden that will not be made known. What I do tell you in the dark, speak it in daylight; what is whispered in your ear, proclaim it from the roofs!" "I did not come to bring peace, but a sword. For it I come to turn!" "If anyone won't welcome you or listen your words, shake the dust off your feet; when you leave that home or town. I tell you truely; it will be more bearable fore Sodom and Gomorrah on the day of judgment then fore that town."

Quotes from The Holy Bible

God bless USA!

And thank you God and Jesus the King and Lord – with all power in Heaven and on earth.

USA IS THE WHITE HORSE IN REVEALTION BOOK IN BIBLE.

"From now I God create something new - you shall not be able to say this I new from before - but don't you see it you can all do so it is already growing up..."

"The word of the Lord came to me: Son of Man; take a stick of wood and write on it: Belonging to Judah tribe. Then take another stick of wood and write on it: belonging to Joseph tribe. Then join them together in "one stick" – that they become one in your hand. This will mean I the Lord do unite in the latest days Judah tribe with Joseph's make them together the Heavenly Kingdom to be ruled by King David as King.". Judah tribe here is Israel and Joseph's tribe is USA. "On that day I will give Gog a burial place in Israel..." "So it will be called the walley of Hamon Gog." "Son of man, prophesy against Gog and say: "This is what Lord says: I am against you! O Gog, Chief prince of Meshesh and Tubal. I will turn you around and drag you along. I will strike your bow from your left hand and let your arrows drop from your right hand. On the mountains of Isreal you will fall, you and all your troups and the nations with you. I will send on Magog and on those who live in the coastlands, and they will know I am the LORD!" "Then those who live in the towns of Israel will go out and use the weapons for fuel and burn them up - the small and large shields, the bows and arrows." "For seven years they will use Magog and his hourd as fuel." "This I will name the Valley of Hamon Gog. Also a town named Hamonah will be there." "Thereafter fore all time to be that way - and my servant David will be King over Israel fore all eternity, and

Israel will have only one King and and one Sheapherd, and David my servant will be one King ruling fore all eternity. My dwelling-place will be with them: I the Lord alone will be their God, and they will be my people. Then the nations will know that I the LORD make Israel holy, when my sanctuary is among them fore ever!" The Heavenly Kingdom of Jesus Christ been under creation fore more then 200 years just now - it is written in Holy Bible in Isaiah: "From now I do create something new - don't you recognize it - it is already grewing up!". It is prophesy about the coming Heavenly Kingdom how God will let the new earth be created the Heavnly Kingdom of Jesus Christ and is the USA. Also the white horse in revelation book. But at the same time after the big beast been thrown in Hell in 1945 there is going to come a little beast too that take power from the big beast and is in it self just little country or even just a city - it came up from the sea - the lake of fire and going to return back to the lake of fire. Just as the boarders around the Heavenly Kingdom of Jesus Christ already been created a - Hell is also been created on earth. The end of end is a war against Gog and Magog and Gog and Magog be thrown in Hell - but the town named Hamonah in Ezekiel it self shall be the boarders around Hell how look like it all there is needed in the sea or lake of fire and the duty at last fore the USA is to throw in to the lake of fire included - being there.

THAT IS THE END OF THE END AFTER THAT THE STARS SHALL FALL DOWN FROM HEAVEN AND SUN TURN AWAY AND MOON TOO - AND THE SIGN OF JESUS CHRIST THE HOLY CROSS WILL APPEAR IN THE SKY. THEN JESUS CHRIST COMES VISIABLE FORE ALL FLESH AND THE PARADISE THEN AFTER THE DOOM BE REALITY FORE ALL TIME. AND BOARDERS AROUND THE NEW EARTH ALREADY "BEEN GROWING UP" - JESUS HEAVENLY KINGDOM. THAT IS THE WHOLE STORY TO COME IN NEAR FUTURE. NO TIME LIMIT ALMOST. "FIRE!" A VERY OLD EXPRESSION AND COMMAND IS SOUNDING JUST NOW BY OUR LORD JESUS CHRIST HIM SELF: IT IS THE VERY LAST COMMAND IN THIS AND IS A COMMAND DIRECTED TO GOD'S AND JESUS HEAVENLY KINGDOM THE USA JUST NOW. GOD WILL ALWAYS ETERNELY BLESS THE USA AND ISRAEL! THEY ARE BOTH TOGETHER THE UNITED STICK IN GOD'S HAND. (COMPARE EZ. 37 AND SO ON). GOD BLESS AMERICA AND ISRAEL AND THE EXPRESSION BE TRUE: "STARS AND STRIPES FORE EVER!" - NO EVER END OF IT NOT EVER. AMEN. THE GRACE OF OUR LORD JESUS CHRIST BLESS THOSE TWO NATIONS FORE ALL TIME TO COME. ETERNELY. GOD'S AND JESUS HEAVENLY KINGDOM. GOD BLESS USA AND ISRAEL! JESUS CHRIST OUR LORD IS UNDER RETURN AND WILL CLOSE THE TIME AND THE HEAVENLY KINGDOM FORE GOD'S CHILDREN TO INHERIT NOW VERY SOON. JUST SOME FEW PARTS LEFT IN ALL PROPHESIES GIVEN IN HOLY BIBLE LEFT. AND JUST WAIT NOW FORE ONE FINAL COMMAND FROM OUR LORD JESUS CHRIST HIM SELF THE COMMAND: FIRE! AFTER THAT FINAL

COMMAND - ALL THE AGES BE CLOSED BY JESUS CHRIST HIM SELF AS HE HAS PROMISED TO DO THEN. "AND LOOK I AM WITH YOU ALL THE AGES UNTIL I CLOSE THE AGE!" QUOTE: JESUS CHRIST MATTHEW.

ISRAEL IS GOING TO BE ATTACKED BY MANY NATIONS INCL. RUSSIA - AND IT GOING TO END UP IN ARMANGEDDON SOON TO COME. AND JESUS DO SAY HIMSELF IN MATTHEW THAT HE IS GOING FIRST TO DEVIDE NATIONS AND ONLY TWO IS GOING TO BE DEVIDED FROM THE REST THE REST END IN HAMON - THE LAKE OF FIRE" - BY DROPS OF HYDROGENIC BOMBS FROM ISRAEL. IS ALSO WRITTEN IN ISIAHA; "FROM NOW I THE LORD DO CREATE SOMETHING NEW - DON'T YOU RECOGNIZE IT IT IS ALREADY GROWING UP.ALSO IT IS WRITTEN IN PETERS SECOND LETTER: "THE FIRST TIME THE WORLD SHALL BE PUNISHED BY WATER THE SECOND TIME BY FIRE!" - AND JESUS ALSO SAYS IN MATTHEW:"WHEN THE SON OF MAN IN THE HEAVEN WITH ALL HIS ANGELS AND SAVED THE UNIVERSE FORCES SHALL BE ROCKED AND THE STARS SHALL ALL FALL DOWN - AND THE SUN SHALL TURN WAY AND THE MOON SHALL TURN TO BLOOD"

"HEAVEN AND EARTH SHALL BOTH DISAPPEAR BUT MY WORDS SHALL ALWAYS BE"

"THEN IT SHALL APPEAR A WHITE THRONE WITH A KING JESUS CHRIST SITTING ON IT WITH A SWORD OF FIRE IN

HIS RIGHT HAND AND WITH THAT SHALL SET A DOOM
OWER BOTH LIVING AND DEAD - THEY ON LEFT SIDE OF
HIM HE SHALL STRIKE WITH THE SWORD OF FIRE AND
THROUGH THEM ALL IN HELL TOGETHER WITH HITLER
THE FALSE PROPHET (THE POPE) AND WITH SATAN AND
HIS ANGELS AND BURN THERE IN ETERNAL SUFFER FOR
ALL TIME TO COME NO EVER END OF IT FOR EVER BURN
IN THE LAKE OF FIRE HAMON. AND ALSO A TOWN SHALL
BE THERE NAMED: HAMONAH

AMEN.

ZERO POINT ONE ZERO POINT ZERO - POINT ZERO - ONE
POINT ZERO= THE END OF THE END - THE ARMANGEDON -
NOW COMPARE EZEKIEL IN THE HOLY BIBLE.

IT IS THEN MENTIONED A BIG BEAST IT WAS NAZI
GERMANY BUT IT IS ALSO MENTIONED AFTER THAT A
LITTLE BEAST THAT SHALL TAKE POWER FROM THE BIG
BEAST AND COME OUT OF THE EARTH. IN EZEKIEL IS
ALSO WRITTEN ABOUT THE COMING THEN
ARMANGEDDON - IT IS TUBAL AND MESHEC THAT IS
NAMES OF RUSSIA AND RUSSIA SHALL GO TO ATTACK
AGAINST THIS UNIFICATION - THE RESULT WILL BE THAT
THEY WILL BE ATTACKED BY WEAPONS OF FIRE AS
WRITTEN IN EZEKIEL - BY THE JEWISH PEOPLE AND
BURN FOR ALL TIME IN THE LAKE OF FIRE AND IN ADD IT

IS MENTIONED THERE SHALL ALSO BE A TOWN THERE NAMED: HAMONAH - WHAT THE MEANING BY THIS IS IS THAT IT SHALL BE A TOWN THAT SHALL BE THE BOARDERS AROUND THE THEN CREATED HELL - HELL IS IN THE LAKE OF FIRE - AND RUSSIA SHALL BE THERE AND AROUND THAT A TOWN NAMED HAMONAH. THE WHOLE PLACE OF ETERNAL PAIN IS NAMED IN EZEKIEL AS THE WALLEY OF HAMON. THAT WAS FROM THE HOLY BIBLE PARTS TELLING ABOUT THE SOON RETURN OF JESUS CHRIST - MESSAIAH.

THAT IS THE END OF THE END AFTER THAT THE STARS SHALL FALL DOWN FROM HEAVEN AND SUN TURN AWAY AND MOON TOO - AND THE SIGN OF JUSUS CHRIST THE HOLY CROSS WILL APPEAR IN THE SKY. THEN JESUS CHRIST COMES VISIABLE FORE ALL FLESH AND THE PARADISE THEN AFTER THE DOOM BE REALITY FORE ALL TIME.   THAT IS THE WHOLE STORY TO COME IN NEAR FUTURE. NO TIME LIMIT ALMOST. GOD WILL ALWAYS ETERNELY BLESS ISRAEL! JESUS CHRIST OUR LORD IS UNDER RETURN AND WILL CLOSE THE TIME AND THE HEAVENLY KINGDOM FORE GOD'S CHILDREN TO INHERIT NOW VERY SOON. JUST SOME FEW PARTS LEFT IN ALL PROPHESIES GIVEN IN HOLY BIBLE LEFT. ALL THE AGES BE CLOSED BY JESUS CHRIST HIM SELF AS HE HAS PROMISED TO DO THEN. SOON THE LAST TRUMPHET WILL SOUND AND THAT PROCLAIM THE SECOND COMING OF JESUS CHRIST AND THEY WILL ALL WHO HAS FOLLOWED JESUS HERE MEET HIM WHEN HE COMES UP

IN THE SKY AND BE IN HEAVEN FOR ALL TIME. AMEN
"AND LOOK I AM WITH YOU ALL THE AGES UNTIL I CLOSE
THE AGE!" QUOTE: JESUS CHRIST MATTHEW. "BLESSED
BE THOSE WHO DO BLESS YOU: ISRAEL!"

MY LIFE AS A CHRISTIAN

By: Leif Krogstad

I became baptized – barried with Jesus in the baptism in
Betel Pentecostal meeting 20th of September 1987 – I
became clinically dead in 1983. I became clinically dead
as I mention and met God and Jesus. And was of mercy
given salvation and reborn on the 8th of July 1983 on
Airport on my way Hospital where I should be transported
to the department that healed damages I still had on the
body - but had until then from the 24th of June been at a
Main Hospital for operation – big operation it was and very
difficult but very good doctors and they managed against
all odds. – but I even became declared dead but was
clinically dead – and was in the death – and met God and
Jesus there among other things that did happen – saw my
life as on a TV-Screen pass by at first the last that
happened was that both God and Jesus were there and

they said: "What shall we do with Leif?" It was said more then once. Then all of a sudden I was back to life in the hospital bed.

Singing; "HOW GREAT THOUGH ARE!" that song a praise song nothing else did fit at all none of the songs from a Agriculture Christian School did fit there and then. And got reborn and got salvation on the 8th of July 1983.

And I do know that the whole bible is God's words and it is true and to be followed and that Jesus is alive and doing that for us give us salvation – God, Jesus and Holy spirits work alone. That gods words in the Bible is the complete truth for us and that the Bible is Holy. God met me there and Jesus at the airport the 8th of July 1983 when I said yes: "Jesus come in to my heart I want to be your child!".

And all of a sudden God's Holy Spirit filled me complete and God talked Prophetic through me for everyone who was at the airport could hear it was like thunder in the voice I was lying down to be carried in to the ambulance to take me to hospital and the quotes where from the Holy Bible:

"In the last days, God says, I will pour out my Spirit over all people, Your sons and daughters will prophesy, your young men will see visions, you old men will dream dreams. Even on my servants, both men and women. I will pour out my Spirit in those days, and they will prophesy. I will show wonders in the heaven above and signs on the earth below, blood and fire and billows smoke. The sun will be turned to darkness and the moon to blood, before the coming of the great and glorious day of the Lord. And everyone that calls the name of the Lord will be saved."

I never had read it any place - not read so much as a word from The Bible before that time.

It is written in The Holy Bible in the old Gospel but also in Acts: in Acts repeated of Peter the Rock - and it is also written that it is in the very last times that shall happen -

"that God will pour out his Spirit over all people!" - and Pentecostal movement did grow up because it did happen first time in the USA among poor people there - it was in the year of 1907 it did happen in USA – the prophesy fulfilled and it is in the end of time it shall happen it is written in The Bible. Or as Jesus Christ do say: "In the close of time!". And it will happen very soon that the end do come after that - and now 2008 - 100 years has gone since then - but still we are living in the very last days and the return of Jesus Christ were he shall judge the whole human kind - still living and those who are dead too. And divide evildoers from the righteous. But there are only one way to be named righteous and it is by take Jesus into the heart - no other way there is to salvation. Because only he is to 100% righteous - none else at all. And we are given by mercy righteousness and salvation through Jesus and Holy Spirits work alone so none have any reason to say: I am myself righteous - because none is. Except Jesus and God.

And from Isaiha in the old Gospel quote: "From now I create something new – don't you recognize it? It is already growing up.

Until then I hadn't even read in The Bible of anything of that very little as a matter of fact read in The Bible – but had had a child belief since I was 3 years old. After that I was carried in to the ambulance and got the permission to talk inside me directly to God and Jesus. And I did then say: "What is really this?" "I heard all the time: non can know God and Jesus do exist! How then this???" Answer:

"There is no problem at all knowing that we do exist everyone can know that!".

And in 1984 when I went a Agricultural School – a Christian School – to get to become a Agronom – had gone Pure Agricultural School at first to become a farmer between 1981 and 1982 – at I went to this Agricultural School because I searched after God and Jesus. I at that time I used to go to each meeting at that School it was a Christian School. But still not got salvation or being born again. One day early in the spring at this School I went out for a walk it was mild temperature outside and no wind at all – it was late in the evening and it was dark. Then I begged in my suffering in longing after knowing if God and Jesus is the truth. "If you are the truth then give me a sign God!" I prayed. All of a sudden in the sky just over the treetops there was lightened up a round light in yellow, I wondered – then an other one was lighten up the same way – looked like lights on a car – but up in the sky – and after that a third one; one after the other horizontally three lights in different colors – then a light was shown over that one that was in the middle: Then I thought if one in add now under the others are lightened up – it becomes a cross! all they were in different colors; and it did a fifth light was lightened up so it made a cross showing – very big could almost seems like an airplane was about to crash but the light did stand complete still and I stood watching for a long time. Then I thought maybe it is a UFO – and then I walked back to the internate – and the belief it was a UFO I did keep fore long time I had seen didn't end believing just that until 1983 8/7 – when God told: "It was a sign from me my child – you begged to me to give you one and it was given!". Is also written in bible beg and you shall be given.

In 1981 to 1984 I got anorexia but God did remove that in one day in 10th of November 1984 – after that never had it – I was only 46 kg and I am 180 cm tall and in 3 weeks I was in normal weight had to eat for three weeks and became 76 kg that is normal and God and Jesus helped my – by his wound you get healthy from sickness is also written. And 8th of July 1983 I got salvation from God and Jesus as mentioned.

When we were on an educational journey at the
Agricultural School in 1985 I went to Philadelphia – a
pentecostal church on meeting one day. After that
because I was a youth and begun at an education: Office
related and became Account Manager in 1988.

In September 1987 I had gone out of the Lutheranian Jew hateress church – this I do say because Luther has written scrips that made almost each country that had Lutheranian belief to be filled with Jew hatetress through history in Europe even used by Hitler those scripts and I wanted to become a member in the Pentecostal movement and be barried in the baptism with Jesus. Then I phoned to Betel – an other Pentecostal church and ask if they could baptize me – complete under the water – as it is done and told in the Bible to do. And The Bible is to a 100% truth that I do know.

Also because that I on the 8th of July 1983 when I got
salvation from God and Jesus - they spoke through me
prophetic quotes from The Holy Bible that I never before in
my whole life until then had read or heard at any point. But
read it afterwards.

Read much in the Bible after that time and do still do so.
Know it is God's Holy word's each inch of it and the
complete truth is in it to be told.

I became a personal Pentecostal Christian the 8th of July 1983 – I went baptised in the grave with Jesus Christ the 20th of September 1987 in Betel Pentecostal Church in Trondheim, Norway and came in touch as early as 1984 with Aage Samuelsen and was in his movement from then he gave me advice to join Pentecostal church of Trondheim – and 15th of November 1987 I got baptised in the Holy Spirit at Aages meeting in turnhallen Oslo – just now I am about to join Pentecostal movement of Norway – central in Oslo by 14th of March 2009. To meet Jesus and God and get salvation be reborn as a Christian is the biggest happening in my life and never will be otherwise – can't ever. End this spelling with these words: None comes to the Father without by Jesus!" And thank you God and

Jesus the King and Lord – with all power in Heaven and on earth.

The Pentecostal Movement in Norway was started by Pastor Thomas B. Barratt with a break through in 1907. To day there is about 280 local Pentecostal churches and over 40.000 members. Thomas T. Barrat (Scottish), and Pioneer Aage Samuelsen - both with great importance even world wide fore Pentecostal church.

It was only a positive attitude and the local movement Pentecostal was blessed with the presence of the Lord himself and the Holy spirit – after being baptized in Betel I became a member at once – they did write me in at the same time as a member and that I should continue to be until 1990.

After this baptism that is urgently necessary for all human beings – there and then it came God spoke through me in Israeli language – ended with I fell on my knees saying Maran-Ata! Maran-Ata! Hallelujah! Hallelujah! The complete ending of it was :"Jesus is here, Jesus is here – Jesus from Nazareth is here." Then it ended. But the same day I was barried with Jesus in the baptism i Betel. I became then a member there the 20th of September 1987.

Pentecostal confession says that bible 100% true and I do know it is the case - I do not believe in God and Jesus I know they are the truth – and Islam most evil organization on earth and has only to be complete forbidden and removed for all time from earth before Christ do come back to judge the world - and that is in no time limit just now in July 2008. About 100 years since the mentioned prophesy was fulfilled that is written in Bible and Pentecostal movement came as direct result - and now no time limit left but Islam has to be complete defeated and removed for all time from earth at first - as criminal organization - if not they anyway got a mighty judgment to meet in no time limit in front of us just now. Also Buddhism and Hinduism and what ever may be just big lies.

But Islam biggest lie - but also the other is lies only –
reincarnation never any time happened to anyone is
written in The Holy Bible:

"It's each human beings destiny one time to die and
thereafter doom!".

And that's clearly words enough just about that matter itself. But is written also in Bible about Mohammed he is mentioned in revelation of John - Jesus disciple - as: "The false prophet to come!" - and what also Islam done - put even a Mosque in Jerusalem and written all around the socket of that Mosque: "God has no Son!" and that almost worse blaspheme ever occur and should be removed that mosque from Jerusalem fore all time to come as fast as possible. Should been done very fast. And what happen everyone has to face Jesus after death and then be judged no matter who and two possible results of these doom then end up in Heaven of Hell - no other way is. And Jesus say himself: "None do come to the Father without through me!" - also written:

"There is no other name ever mentioned to get salvation through then God's son Jesus!".

Paul says that in Bible. And I know there are no other way for anyone no matter what has of belief on earth all meet Jesus after death - all happen to everyone no exception – no way ever to escape from that: "One time to die thereafter doom" is as mentioned written in bible and know it is true.

Islam really bad religion - as a matter of fact no religion at all - just a criminal organization - one of the biggest lies ever told – only Christianity is the complete truth - nothing else - Jesus is the truth in person himself - no matter what humans may believe there are only one real truth and this truth is Jesus Christ himself none else - this I really not believe I know it - and not difficult at all in world of today to know just that - for instance just take a look at the Corp. sheet of Torino and what is found out about it - no leave for doubt then - even Jesus said: "I shall give you only one sign after me: The Jonah Sign!" - That was in itself that he did rise from death to life and is the only King ruling and got all power in Heaven and on earth - this is the truth and Bible is truth all of it - God's words it is - spoken to humanity given them as a treasure and a gift – until Jesus do return and will judge all humankind - what Islam concern will get a very hard doom by Christ no doubt either ever to have in that matter - but we humans can even have it forbidden to exist on earth because it as organization brakes almost all of UN's declaration of human rights and that's only fact - truly they soon gonna face reality all of them and everyone who do die cause they all are set to face Christ himself without exception... Because he has always been the only truth..

"But whoever causes the one of these little ones who believe in Me to sin, it would be better for him if a millstone were hung around his neck, and he were drowned in the depth of the sea!"

(Matthew 18,6)

I do know The Bible has the complete message to human kind from Jesus Christ himself. It is long time ago given prophesies in the Gospel Old and also in Now repeated what happened at Pentecostal time - it did come through in 1907 in The USA – it happened there first. And brought to the rest of the world - as early as in 1907.

I met God and Jesus and got salvation 8th of July and I am from that time a Christian and believe in the Bible to a hundred percent - it is written the complete truth there and believe in God and Jesus and that Jesus is King and Lord - and son of God. That be the complete truth told in Bible – Jesus do live and do rule both Heaven and earth - Jesus says himself: "Me is given all power both in Heaven and on earth and I be with you till the close of age!"

And thank you God and Jesus the King and Lord – with all power in Heaven and on earth.

God's rich blessing to the Pentecostal Movement in New York and Florida and Oslo Pentecostal Church, Norway. God and Jesus Christ be with you all and follow you wherever you may walk on the way of life – Only Jesus is the way, the whole truth and the life itself – none come to the father without by Jesus. Thanks to you all and bless you all i our in Jesus name – our Lord and King – none else has all the power and is the complete truth then Jesus and the Bible is Holy – it is God speaking in it to a 100% the Bible is truth. To meet Jesus and God and get salvation be reborn as a Christian is the biggest happening in my life and never will be otherwise – can't ever. End this spelling with these words: None comes to the Father without by Jesus!

"When the Son of man comes in his glory, and all the angels with him, then he will sit on his glorious throne. Before him will be gathered all the nations, and he will separate them one from another as a shepherd separates the sheep from the goats, and he will place the sheep at his right hand, but the goats at the left. Then the King will say to those at his right hand, "Come, O blessed of my Father, inherit the kingdom prepared for you from the foundation of the world; for I was hungry and you gave me food, I was thirsty and you gave me drink, I was a stranger and you welcomed me, I was naked and you clothed me, I was sick and you visited me, I was in prison and you came to me." Then the righteous will answer him, "Lord, when did we see the hungry and feed thee, or thirsty and give thee drink? And when did we see thee a stranger and welcome thee, or naked and clothe thee? And when did we see thee sick or in prison and visit thee?" And the King will answer them, "Truly, I say to you, as you did it to one of the least of these my brethren, you did it to me." Then he will say to those at his left hand, "Depart from me, you cursed, into the eternal fire prepared for the devil and his angels; for I was hungry and you gave me no food, I was thirsty and you gave me no drink, I was a stranger and you did not welcome me, naked and you did not clothe me, sick and in prison and you did not visit me." Then they also will answer, "Lord, when did we see thee hungry or thirsty or a stranger or naked or sick or in prison, and did not minister to thee?" Then he will answer them, 'Truly, I say to you, as you did it not to one of the least of these, you did it not to me." And they will go away into eternal punishment, but the righteous into eternal life.

THEY IT IS GIVEN TAKES INTO THEIR HEART WHAT THE SPIRIT SAYS TO THE CHILDREN OF MANKIND

Quotes: The Holy bible.

Very soon now Jesus is going to return and that is the end of the end.

THE END OF THE END THE EMPIRE OF JESUS CHIRST TO COME - SOON!

"And I saw a Beast coming out of sea.... That beast was killed and thrown in the Lake of fire and by the King riding the white horse – but is then following setting "And then I saw an other beast, coming out of the earth" – the power the last beast has it takes from the first – and the King riding the white horse did destroy also this last beast and throw it all in the lake of fire where the first beast already is and just one thing left then to take the beast that came out of earth and then create the complete work – command to do so by Jesus Christ – at last after the doom set. The King on the white horse: Jesus Christ - by command: "Devide et impera" – then this little part – the little beast on earth be all thrown in Hell and creation of Hell fore all evil creatures to be for all time in eternal pain and punishement – no ever end of it when the last beast killed and the Devil who do rules that last location as a country or a city be determinated for all time all it fore all time to come by the sword of fire in the hand of the King of Kings Jesus Christ. " "Concerning the coming of the Lord Jesus Christ , that day will not come until the rebellion occurs and the man of lawlessness is revealed, the man doomed to destruction. He will oppose and will exalt himself over that is named God or us worshipped - and even proclaim himself to be God!" "And now you can know who is holding him back, so he may be revealed at the proper time. For the secret power of the lawlessness is already at work. And then the lawless one will be revealed; whom the Lord Jesus will overthrow complete - determinate. The grace of our Lord Jesus Christ be with you all and defend you in the power of God's Holy Spirit. (2 Thes. 2)Then only one word left for the King to say: "The Heavenly Kingom is now completed and it is just fore you be children and to take part of your herritage that been prepared for you before the creation itself!"God and Jesus always has ruled all there is. "

"Listen, I will tell you a mystery! We will not all die but we will be changed. In a moment, in the twinkling of an eye, at the last trumpet. Fore the trumpet will sound, and the dead will be raised imperishable bodies must be put on immortaly." 1 Cor 15

"Fore the Lord himself, with a cry of command, with the archangels call and the sound of God's trumpet, will descend from Heaven, and the dead in Christ will rise first. Then we who are alive who are left, will be caught up in the clouds together with them to meet the Lord in the air. Then we will be with the Lord for ever!" 2 Thes 4

THE END OF END - THE CLOSE OF THE AGES: RETURN OF THE KING OF KINGS

"And soon our King Jesus Christ is going return to judge all flesh – all human kind as King and judge at judgment day – when he do close the age and we the Kingdom of Heaven for all eternity. The New Jerusalem to inherit for eternity to come no end of it. And meet all our beloved ones there. Then the King of Kings will say: Now the time is closed! Very soon now Jesus is going to return and that is the end of the end.".

"On that day I will give Gog a burial place in Israel..." "So it will be called the walley of Hamon Gog." "Son of man, prophesy against Gog and say: "This is what Lord says: I am against you! O Gog, Chief prince of Meshesh and Tubal. I will turn you around and drag you along. I will strike your bow from your left hand and let your arrows drop from your right hand. On the mountains of Isreal you will fall, you and all your troups and the nations with you. I will send on Magog and on those who live in the coastlands, and they will know I am the LORD!" "Then those who live in the towns of Israel will go out and use the weapons for fuel and burn them up - the small and large shields, the bows and arrows." "For seven years they will use Magog and his hourd as fuel." "This I will name the Valley of Hamon Gog. Also a town named Hamonah will be there." "Thereafter for all time to be that way - and my servant David will be King over Israel fore all eternity, and Israel will have only one King and and one Sheapherd, and David my servant will be one King ruling fore all eternity. My dwelling-place will be with them: I the Lord alone will be their God, and they will be my people. Then the nations will know that I the LORD make Israel holy, when my sanctuary is among them for ever!" But at the same time after the big beast been thrown in Hell in 1945 there is going to come a little beast too that take power from the big beast and is in it self just little country or even just a city - it came up from the sea - the lake of fire and going to return back to the lake of fire. The end of end is a war against Gog and Magog and Gog and Magog be thrown in Hell - but the town named Hamonah in Ezekiel the boarders around Hell how look like it all there is needed in the sea or lake of fire.

THAT IS THE END OF THE END AFTER THAT THE STARS SHALL FALL DOWN FROM HEAVEN AND SUN TURN AWAY AND MOON TOO – AND THE SIGN OF JESUS CHRIST THE HOLY CROSS WILL APPEAR IN THE SKY. THEN JESUS WILL COME.THAT IS THE WHOLE STORY TO COME IN NEAR FUTURE. NO TIME LIMIT ALMOST. GOD WILL ALWAYS ETERNELY BLESS ISRAEL!

JESUS CHRIST OUR LORD IS UNDER RETURN AND WILL CLOSE THE TIME AND THE HEAVENLY KINGDOM FOR GOD'S CHILDREN TO INHERIT NOW VERY SOON. JUST SOME FEW PARTS LEFT IN ALL PROPHESIES GIVEN IN HOLY BIBLE LEFT. AFTER THAT ALL THE AGES BE CLOSED BY JESUS CHRIST HIM SELF AS HE HAS PROMISED TO DO THEN. "AND LOOK I AM WITH YOU ALL

THE AGES UNTIL I CLOSE THE AGE!" QUOTE: JESUS
CHRIST MATTHEW.

"BLESSED BE THOSE WHO DO BLESS YOU: ISRAEL!"

First shall happen due to Ezekiel that the Temple shall be
rebuilt in Israel.

"And I saw, and behold a white horse: and he that sat on
him had a bow; and a crown was given unto him: and he
went for conquering, and to conquer. And I saw heaven
opened, and behold a white horse; and he that sat upon
him was called Faithful and True, and in righteousness he
doth judge and make war. And the He fought agains the
False Prophet at last - and the False Prophet was thrown
in Gahenna... And the rest of them were all killed with the
sword of fire in the hand by the King riding the white
horse. Then I saw a great white throne and the King of
Kings was seated on and crowned he is - and each person
was jugded according to what they had done.... And the
devil was thrown into the lake of eternal fire and eternal
suffer... Then death and Hades were thrown in the lake of
fire... And if anyone's name was not found, he was thrown
into the lake of fire and eternal suffer forever devided from
God's people..."

 Last in Ezekiel 37 a.s.o. it is descriebed a war against
Israel – all nations going to be a part of it but main is
Russia and EU – EU is the Beast in Revelation book of John
– it got a deadly wound when Adolph Hitler lost the war–
he killed 6 million Jews – the pearl in the eye of God – and
Germany never is forgiven for that and shall be punished –

but that wound got healed by the unification of the evil Germany in 1990 by this unification. UK and Israel is going to use all their atom weapons in this war it is written that the Israeli people is going to defend themselves by weapons of fluel. And only Norway, UK and Israel is going to be left on earth. At the same time Jesus do return and we who are Christians going to meet him up in the sky and the world will burn down and a new earth and a new heaven will appear where rightoesness do rule for all time and we are going to live in the New Jerusalem for all time.

The False Prophet in Revelation book is Mohammed - he name himself as misguiding the "last prophet". Amen

"On that day I will give Gog a burial place in Israel..." "So it will be called the walley of Hamon Gog." "Son of man, prophesy against Gog and say: "This is what Lord says: I am against you! O Gog, Chief prince of Meshesh and Tubal. I will turn you around and drag you along. I will strike your bow from your left hand and let your arrows drop from your right hand. On the mountains of Isreal you will fall, you and all your troups and the nations with you. I will send on Magog and on those who live in the coastlands, and they will know I am the LORD!" "Then those who live in the towns of Israel will go out and use the weapons fore fuel and burn them up - the small and large shields, the bows and arrows." "For seven years they will use Magog and his hourd as fuel." "This I will name the Valley of Hamon Gog.

Also a town named Hamonah will be there." "Thereafter fore all time to be that way - and my servant David will be King over Israel fore all eternity, and Israel will have only one King and and one Sheapherd, and David my servant will be one King ruling fore all eternity. My dwelling-place will be with them: I the Lord alone will be their God, and they will be my people. Then the nations will know that I the LORD make Israel holy, when my sanctuary is among them fore ever!" The end of end is a war against Gog and Magog and Gog and Magog be thrown in Hell - but the town named Hamonah in Ezekiel is Namsos in Norway and it self shall be the boarders around Hell how look like it all there is needed in the sea or lake of fire and is to throw in to the lake of fire included - being there.

ISRAEL IS GOING TO BE ATTACKED BY MANY NATIONS INCL. RUSSIA - AND IT GOING TO END UP IN ARMANGEDDON SOON TO COME. AND JESUS DO SAY HIMSELF IN MATTHEW THAT HE IS GOING FIRST TO DEVIDE NATIONS AND ONLY TWO IS GOING TO BE DEVIDED FROM THE REST THE REST END IN HAMON - THE LAKE OF FIRE" - BY DROPS OF HYDROGENIC BOMBS FROM ISRAEL. IS ALSO WRITTEN IN ISIAHA; "FROM NOW I THE LORD DO CREATE SOMETHING NEW - DON'T YOU RECOGNIZE IT IT IS ALREADY GROWING UP.ALSO IT IS WRITTEN IN PETERS SECOND LETTER: "THE FIRST TIME THE WORLD SHALL BE PUNISHED BY WATER THE SECOND TIME BY FIRE!" - AND JESUS ALSO SAYS IN MATTHEW:"WHEN THE SON OF MAN IN THE HEAVEN

WITH ALL HIS ANGELS AND SAVED THE UNIVERSE
FORCES SHALL BE ROCKED AND THE STARS SHALL ALL
FALL DOWN - AND THE SUN SHALL TURN WAY AND THE
MOON SHALL TURN TO BLOOD"

"HEAVEN AND EARTH SHALL BOTH DISAPPEAR BUT MY
WORDS SHALL ALWAYS BE"

"THEN IT SHALL APPEAR A WHITE THRONE WITH A KING
JESUS CHRIST SITTING ON IT WITH A SWORD OF FIRE IN
HIS RIGHT HAND AND WITH THAT SHALL SET A DOOM
OWER BOTH LIVING AND DEAD - THEY ON LEFT SIDE OF
HIM HE SHALL STRIKE WITH THE SWORD OF FIRE AND
THROUGH THEM ALL IN HELL TOGETHER WITH HITLER
THE FALSE PROPHET (MOHAMMED) AND WITH SATAN
AND HIS ANGELS AND BURN THERE IN ETERNAL SUFFER
FOR ALL TIME TO COME NO EVER END OF IT FOR EVER
BURN IN THE LAKE OF FIRE HAMON. AND ALSO A TOWN
SHALL BE THERE NAMED: HAMONAH

AMEN.

ZERO POINT ONE ZERO POINT ZERO - POINT ZERO - ONE
POINT ZERO= THE END OF THE END - THE ARMANGEDON -
NOW COMPARE EZEKIEL IN THE HOLY BIBLE.

IT IS THEN MENTIONED A BIG BEAST IT WAS NAZI
GERMANY BUT IT IS ALSO MENTIONED AFTER THAT A
LITTLE BEAST THAT SHALL TAKE POWER FROM THE BIG
BEAST AND COME OUT OF THE EARTH. IN EZEKIEL IS
ALSO WRITTEN ABOUT THE COMING THEN
ARMANGEDDON - IT IS TUBAL AND MESHEC THAT IS
NAMES OF RUSSIA AND RUSSIA SHALL GO TO ATTACK
AGAINST THIS UNIFICATION - THE RESULT WILL BE THAT
THEY WILL BE ATTACKED BY WEAPONS OF FIRE AS
WRITTEN IN EZEKIEL - BY THE JEWISH PEOPLE AND
BURN FOR ALL TIME IN THE LAKE OF FIRE AND IN ADD IT
IS MENTIONED THERE SHALL ALSO BE A TOWN THERE
NAMED: HAMONAH - WHAT THE MEANING BY THIS IS IS
THAT IT SHALL BE A TOWN THAT SHALL BE THE
BOARDERS AROUND THE THEN CREATED HELL - HELL IS
IN THE LAKE OF FIRE - AND RUSSIA SHALL BE THERE
AND AROUND THAT A TOWN NAMED HAMONAH. THE
WHOLE PLACE OF ETERNAL PAIN IS NAMED IN EZEKIEL
AS THE WALLEY OF HAMON. THAT WAS FROM THE HOLY
BIBLE PARTS TELLING ABOUT THE SOON RETURN OF
JESUS CHRIST - MESSAIAH.

THAT IS THE END OF THE END AFTER THAT THE STARS
SHALL FALL DOWN FROM HEAVEN AND SUN TURN AWAY
AND MOON TOO - AND THE SIGN OF JUSUS CHRIST THE
HOLY CROSS WILL APPEAR IN THE SKY. THEN JESUS
CHRIST COMES VISIABLE FORE ALL FLESH AND THE
PARADISE THEN AFTER THE DOOM BE REALITY FORE ALL
TIME.   THAT IS THE WHOLE STORY TO COME IN NEAR

FUTURE. NO TIME LIMIT ALMOST. GOD WILL ALWAYS ETERNELY BLESS ISRAEL! JESUS CHRIST OUR LORD IS UNDER RETURN AND WILL CLOSE THE TIME AND THE HEAVENLY KINGDOM FORE GOD'S CHILDREN TO INHERIT NOW VERY SOON. JUST SOME FEW PARTS LEFT IN ALL PROPHESIES GIVEN IN HOLY BIBLE LEFT. ALL THE AGES BE CLOSED BY JESUS CHRIST HIM SELF AS HE HAS PROMISED TO DO THEN. "AND LOOK I AM WITH YOU ALL THE AGES UNTIL I CLOSE THE AGE!" QUOTE: JESUS CHRIST MATTHEW. "BLESSED BE THOSE WHO DO BLESS YOU: ISRAEL!"

"Listen, I will tell you a mystery! We will not all die but we will be changed. In a moment, in the twinkling of an eye, at the last trumpet. Fore the trumpet will sound, and the dead will be raised imperishable bodies must be put on immortaly." 1 Cor 15 "Fore the Lord himself, with a cry of command, with the archangels call and the sound of God's trumpet, will descend from Heaven, and the dead in Christ will rise first. Then we who are alive who are left, will be caught up in the clouds together with them to meet the Lord in the air. Then we will be with the Lord for ever!" 2 Thes 4 THE END OF END - THE CLOSE OF THE AGES: RETURN OF THE KING OF KING

THE END

Leif Krogstad © 2015

www.ingramcontent.com/pod-product-compliance
Lightning Source LLC
Chambersburg PA
CBHW032035090426
42741CB00006B/829